Parson Russell Terrier

By Christine Carter

D1472962

BREEDERS' BEST
A KENNEL CLUB BOOK™

PARSON RUSSELL TERRIER

ISBN: 1-59378-922-X

Copyright © 2004
Kennel Club Books, LLC
308 Main Street, Allenhurst, NJ 07711 USA
Printed in South Korea

PHOTOS BY:
Isabelle Français
and Bernd Brinkmann.

DRAWINGS BY:
Elvira.

Contents

Meet the Parson Russell Terrier

The Parson Russell Terrier (PRT) is an active, robust, intelligent and very bright dog. He is small (below the knee in height) and, weighing less than 20 pounds, he fits nicely into either a city home or a house in the country. Do not let his small size fool you, though, as this is an extremely active dog who likes challenges, requires much activity and needs an owner who is as smart and active as he is!

The PRT is a member of the Terrier Group of dogs. Nearly all of the terrier

By any name, this is a very recognizable dog! Previously known as the Jack Russell Terrier, this popular breed is now officially recognized by the AKC as the Parson Russell Terrier.

breeds originated in the British Isles, and the PRT is no exception. Most short- and medium-legged terriers were bred to go to ground after any kind of pesky vermin that was a nuisance on the farms or in the homes, and the PRT is no exception. As early as 1735, the *Sportsman's Dictionary* wrote that the terrier is "a kind of hound, used only or chiefly for hunting the fox or badger." James Watson wrote in the early 1900s that the terrier was developed from the common material of England and that they were hard-biting, game dogs, small enough to go to earth after the fox and badger. The PRT's purpose was to either outsmart the fox or badger by preventing it from going into its bolt hole or to tease and annoy the animal already hidden underground in order to drive it out to the waiting hounds and hunters. Rarely was he called upon to actually fight, but if that circumstance arose, he was up to the task.

Given the PRT's terrier inquisitiveness, compact size and athleticism, there's not much he can't get into (or out of) when the urge to explore strikes. Safety, both indoors and out, is a major priority for owners of the breed.

The breed's personality is well represented by this dog's alert "what's next?" expression.

The history of the PRT is fairly easy to trace, compared to many of the other terriers, as the breed was developed by John (Jack) Russell, who was born in 1795 and grew up in North Devon, England. From a very early age, he took an interest in dogs and hunting, and, when he was studying at Oxford, he purchased a smart little Fox Terrier bitch from the driver of the local milk wagon. Trump, as she was called, became the foundation stock for the Jack Russell Terrier and it is said that Trump appeared in the background of every Jack Russell Terrier born during the following 50 years.

Russell was ordained a minister, following in his father's footsteps, in 1819. He preached in the neighboring parishes and was a well-liked individual, noted for his kindness and love of animals. In 1873, Russell became a founding member of the English Kennel Club. By that time, it was obvious that there was a split between show-type Fox Terriers and the working terriers that Russell preferred. By the time of his death, in 1883, he was credited with being the "father of Fox Terriers."

Around 1895, the Parson Jack Russell Terrier Club was founded. The club's goal was to "encourage the breeding of the old-fashioned North Devon Fox Terrier, brought to prominence particularly through the terriers bred by the Reverend John Russell." In 1900, the Fox Terrier class was a popular one at dog shows, but the Jack Russell Terrier continued his occupation as a working dog, pursuing his quarry and hunting with his master. By 1925, it was argued in a court of law that the Jack Russell Terrier was a distinct breed and, although not recognized by The Kennel Club of Great Britain, still had considerable value. The judge agreed, as do many show judges today!

At the end of World War II, there were few Jack Russell Terriers being bred. The individuals who still were breeding were forced to cross

This is a true terrier in hunting skill and instinct, along with unfailing courage in going to ground in pursuit of small prey. He's prized by hunters as well as by those who want a good vermin exterminator around the house and farm.

their dogs with Fox Terriers, Dachshunds and Corgis, and even with Sealyham Terriers. The breed became a strange lot, with differences in size, length, height, ear carriage and coat texture. Various Jack Russell clubs appeared, each with its own type of dog that it preferred and recognized. The short-legged type became a wildly popular pet and remains so to this day. Words were exchanged between the various clubs and many negotiations took place between the clubs and The Kennel Club. Finally, in 1997, the Jack Russell Terrier was able to win Challenge Certificates (needed for a British championship) for the first time at a sanctioned show in Britain. The breed is now know as the Parson Russell Terrier in the UK.

Jack Russell Terriers had been imported into the United States, and by 1976 the Jack Russell Terrier Club of America was formed. Today there are now over 3,000 club members, as the breed has become quite popular in America. It is in the top half in popularity of the breeds recognized by the American Kennel Club (AKC), being accepted by the AKC in 1997. Accepted as the Jack Russell Terrier since 1991, the breed continues to be among the most popular dogs with the United Kennel Club (UKC). The breed, originally recognized as the Jack Russell Terrier by the

Regardless of by what name he's known, the PRT has gained a solid reputation around the world as a favorite pet and hunter's companion. This handsome trio hails from Germany.

AKC, officially changed its name to Parson Russell Terrier in April 2003, with the purpose of naming the dog after the individual who was so closely associated with the beginnings of the breed and to remain true to the original longer-legged type developed by Parson Russell. The UKC divided the Jack Russell Terrier into two separate breeds in 2001, when it recognized the shorter-legged variety as the Russell Terrier. For the sake of clarity, we will call the breed Parson Russell Terrier (PRT) throughout this book.

Whether looking for an energetic companion, show dog, an obedience or agility dog or a dog that can work in the field, the Parson Russell Terrier will be an excellent choice. Do remember, however, that this is a smart and active dog who asks that his owner be as smart and ready for adventure as he is. As a PRT owner, you will be required to work with your dog, train him and enjoy him, and you will have a wonderful pet and companion for life.

MEET THE PARSON RUSSELL TERRIER

Overview

- In true terrier fashion, the Parson Russell Terrier was bred to go to ground in pursuit of vermin.
- The "father" of the breed is John "Jack" Russell, an English minister with a love of animals, particularly working terriers, who laid the foundation for the Jack Russell Terrier, today's PRT.
- Divergence in type between show-type and working-type terriers led to the recognition of the working PRT as a distinct breed in England.
- The PRT made its way across the Atlantic and found great favor in the US, where it is now among the most popular breeds.
- Today some countries differentiate between working and show PRTs, classifying them separately under different names.

Description of the PRT

Every breed of dog has an official written standard of perfection, and this standard gives a mental picture of how the ideal representative of the breed should look, act and move. The Parson Russell Terrier's standard is formulated by the national breed club. The Parson Russell Terrier Association of America (formerly known as the Jack Russell Terrier Association of America) is the parent club for the AKC, and you can find that complete standard at the AKC's website (www.akc.org). For the standard approved by the UKC, you

This broken-coated PRT shows natural facial furnishings along with desirable dark eyes, dark pigmentation, small drop ears and "ready-for-anything" expression.

can visit www.ukcdogs.com. The UKC's standard is upheld by such parent clubs as the North American Jack Russell Association and the Jack Russell Terrier Breeders' Association.

The PRT should have a compact, muscular body, always ready to spring into action.

The PRT is a very active, sturdy, fearless and confident terrier who has a strong working instinct and does not show any signs of nervousness or cowardice. His temperament is most essential, and the AKC standard says that he should be "Bold and friendly. Athletic and clever. At work he is a game hunter, tenacious and coura-geous. At home he is playful, exuberant and overwhelmingly affec-tionate. He is an independent and energetic terrier and requires his due portion of attention." The UKC standard includes the following to describe the breed's character: "The Jack Russell Terrier is a bold, friendly, active and alert hunting Terrier, built for work underground. This breed is notoriously fearless and requires little

The erect ear shown here is not acceptable according to the breed standard. The correct ear is the "button" ear, a small drop ear folded over and carried close to the head.

CORRECT	INCORRECT

Correct body in profile.

Dip in topline, no tuck-up.

Roached back and too much tuck-up.

Frontal view of correct head.

Ears too large.

Narrow muzzle and face, lack of cheeks.

Correct head shown in profile.

No stop, blunt muzzle, large ears.

Correct forequarters.

Too-narrow front.

Barrel-chested, too wide.

Correct hindquarters.

Extremely cow-hocked.

Bowlegged and toeing in.

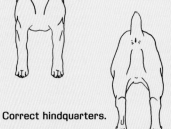

encouragement to go to ground. Aggression toward anything other than legitimate quarry detracts from the dog's ability as a working terrier and should be discouraged as much as possible. This is a high-energy breed and is happiest in an environment where there is lots of regular activity."

In size, the PRT should be between 12 and 14 inches high at the shoulder, and he is of medium size and bone. The UKC standard indicates that dogs can be 10 to 15 inches in height, and divides the dogs into two classes for showing (10 inches to 12.5 inches, and over 12.5 inches to 15 inches). In proper hard condition, the dog weighs between 13 and 17 pounds. It is essential that he have the correct chest size so that he will be able to pursue vermin underground. In addition, he must have suffi-cient leg so that he can be speedy enough to follow the hounds on the hunt.

His head should be in proportion to the rest of his body, and he should have a keen expression that shows intelligence. His eyes are dark and almond-shaped, and his drop ear is carried close to his head. His teeth are large for his size (a trait shared by all terriers) and must be in a correct scissors bite, with the upper teeth overlapping the bottom teeth.

A well-put-together PRT has well-laid-back shoulders, and the forelimbs are placed well under the dog with the elbows hanging perpendicular to the body. His feet are round, compact and cat-like. His hindquarters are strong and muscular.

According to the AKC standard, the PRT has two coat varieties: the smooth, which is coarse and weatherproof, dense and flat; and the broken, which is harsh and dense, with a tendency to curl or wave (never woolly). The broken-coated dog will carry more

Skull: Cranium.

Stop: Indentation between the eyes at point of nasal bones and skull.

Muzzle: Foreface or region of head in front of eyes.

Lip: Fleshy portion of upper and lower jaws.

Occiput: Upper back part of skull; apex.

Topline: Outline from withers to tailset.

Withers: Highest part of the back, at the base of neck above the shoulders.

Shoulder: Upper point of forequarters; the region of the two shoulder blades.

Forechest: Sternum.

Chest: Thoracic cavity (enclosed by ribs).

Forequarters: Front assembly from shoulder to feet.

Upper arm: Region between shoulder blade and forearm.

Elbow: Region where humerus and ulna meet.

Forearm: Region between humerus and wrist.

Carpus: Wrist.

Dewclaw: Extra digit on inside of leg; fifth toe.

Brisket: Lower chest.

Pastern: Region between wrist and toes.

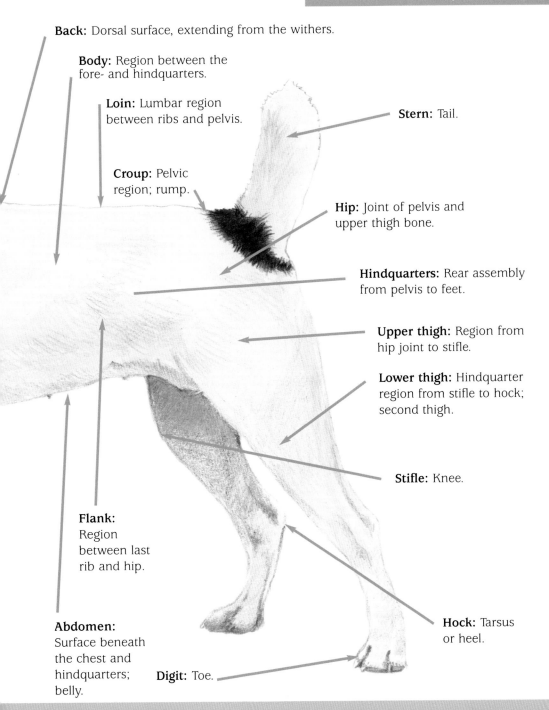

Back: Dorsal surface, extending from the withers.

Body: Region between the fore- and hindquarters.

Loin: Lumbar region between ribs and pelvis.

Stern: Tail.

Croup: Pelvic region; rump.

Hip: Joint of pelvis and upper thigh bone.

Hindquarters: Rear assembly from pelvis to feet.

Upper thigh: Region from hip joint to stifle.

Lower thigh: Hindquarter region from stifle to hock; second thigh.

Stifle: Knee.

Flank: Region between last rib and hip.

Abdomen: Surface beneath the chest and hindquarters; belly.

Digit: Toe.

Hock: Tarsus or heel.

coat than the smooth-coated dog. Both coat types are double coats, meaning a soft undercoat and a harsher outer coat.

The UKC standard lists three coat types, the smooth, rough and the broken, all of which are dense, hard and weather-resistant, covering the entire dog, including the belly and underside of the thighs. The rough coat is described as "a double coat consisting of a short, dense undercoat and very dense, wiry outer coat. Hair over the eyes and on the muzzle will form eyebrows and a beard. The outer coat should not be so long as to obscure the outline of the dog." The UKC uses the term "broken" to refer to an intermediate coat between the smooth and the rough, adding that "the broken coat lies closer to the body than a rough coat and has longer guard hairs than a smooth coat. A broken-coated dog may or may not have face furnishings."

The PRT's colors, including white, white with black and tan markings and tricolor, should be clear, and the markings are usually confined to the head and root of the tail. Heavy markings over the body are not desirable. Grizzle, a mixture of black or red hairs with white hairs, which is different from brindle, is an acceptable color in the breed as well. Brindle (a genetically based color pattern that produces a striping effect) is a disqualification in this breed, though it is common in Fox Terriers. The UKC standard insists on the coat's being at least 50% white.

This is a well-coordinated dog on the move, and gait is one of the most critical tests of a dog's proper construction. The PRT's movement will be free and lively, with good reach and drive and an ample length of stride. His faults are few, but for showing the following apply: Over 15 inches and under 12 inches in height; prick ears; improper bite; chest not spannable; hare feet; woolly coat or lacking undercoat. Brindle markings and shyness are also faults.

It should be noted that, if you plan to work your PRT or show him in the conformation ring, he must be trained to have his chest spanned. The standard notes that the judge should be able to "span with hands tightly behind the elbows on the forward portion of the chest. The chest must be easily spanned by average-size hands. Thumbs should meet at the spine and fingers should meet under the chest." If the judge is unable to span the chest with his hands, the chest is not of the correct size for the dog to go underground and hunt properly.

In addition, the AKC standard notes the following: "Old scars or injuries, the result of work or accident, should not be allowed to prejudice a terrier's chance in the show ring unless they interfere with its movement or with its utility for work or stud."

DESCRIPTION OF THE PRT

Overview

- In the US, the main breed standards for the PRT are set forth by the AKC and the UKC.
- Both standards agree that "bold and friendly" are at the heart of this active, game and courageous terrier's disposition.
- Exact size requirements vary between the two registries, but the PRT is a compact, sturdy dog with proper chest size and leg length for going to ground.
- The PRT can be smooth- or broken-coated, with the UKC further recognizing a rough coat. All coat types should be double-coated and the hair should be harsh, dense and weather-resistant.
- Proper movement indicates proper construction, and the PRT should be quick and agile, with a lively, ample stride.

CHAPTER 3

Are You a PRT Person?

P arson Russell Terriers are hunting dogs, and new owners cannot ignore or forget this basic element of the breed's being. As terriers, they like to dig, can have an aggressive nature and can be prone to bark more than other dogs. Like many small, assertive dogs, PRTs have no concept of their size and act as if they weigh at least 100 pounds. In attitude, PRTs can take on anything that is foolish enough to cross their paths. They can be aggressive with other pets, such as cats or rabbits, which to a PRT are game animals. Overt aggression to people,

As a hunter of vermin by trade, the PRT may mistake other pets in the house for prey! Make introductions carefully and avoid small pets such as hamsters, gerbils, guinea pigs and the like. Most PRTs will get along with cats if properly socialized and supervised as their friendship develops.

livestock or other dogs is a major fault, and responsible breeders are keenly aware of this. In addition, they enjoy good lifespans of up to 15 years, and throughout that time they can remain physically active and challenging.

If you want to have a PRT as a pet, you must be aware of these qualities, which make this breed the unique and wonderful dog it is. Having said this, there is no reason that a well-bred PRT, when owned by a responsible owner who can sensibly train his dog and let the dog know who the boss is, cannot be a simply delightful companion for all of his years.

A smart PRT with a feather in his cap! The Parson Russell Terrier is never all work; he has quite a playful side, too, and enjoys having fun with his family.

Before purchasing your PRT, you must give serious thought to the personality and characteristics of this breed to determine if the PRT is right for you. This is not a dog for the laid-back owner who will not give the dog the training and attention that he deserves. In addition, this is likely not a good choice for the first-time dog owner. This is a dog for the individual

This dog is proud to be a Parson Russell Terrier and isn't shy about telling the world!

who has studied up on the breed, understands its characteristics and is willing to train the dog and give him the time and activity that he requires.

You should answer the following questions before beinning your search for a PRT:

1. Do you have the time to give to a dog? He will need care, companionship, training and grooming. This is almost like having a child, except the dog remains a child and will always require your care. Fortunately, most PRTs do not go off to college, so that's one bill you won't have to worry about!

2. Do you have a fenced yard for your PRT? This is not a breed that you can trust off-lead. He is a runner, and the scent or sight of squirrel or cat will send him flying furiously in the direction of the offending foe. The PRT must have a secure (escape-proof) area

in which to run and exercise.

3. Have you owned a dog previously and did that dog live a long and happy life with you and your family?

4. Do you have small children and are you willing to instruct and supervise them so that they will not mistreat this small but feisty dog?

5. Are you willing and able to have a dog that tends to be a bit noisy? Will your neighbors tolerate this?

6. Even if the PRT requires a minimum of grooming, he will require some coat care. Do you have the time and interest to keep your dog looking like a handsome member of his breed?

Let's look at each question, one at a time.

1. Having time for a dog does not mean that you cannot work and own a dog. Your pet will need quality time, though, just like a child. He must be fed on a regular

daily schedule and exercised several times a day. He needs to be petted and loved, and he will want to spend lots of quality time with you. You must work with him to have an obedient dog who has good manners. Your dog should have at *least* two good outings a day, and that means a walk or a good romp in both the morning and the evening. Never let him out loose to run the neighborhood, as you may not see him again.

2. A securely fenced yard should be of ample size to give you space to throw a ball and for your dog to run with it. And, remember, it is your responsibility to keep the yard clean of dog droppings. When walking your dog, it is essential to carry a plastic bag or two to pick up droppings. These can be easily dropped in a handy trash receptacle on your way home. Most communities have laws about picking up after your dog. Given the clear and present danger of anti-dog laws, all dog owners must act responsibly and be considerate toward their neighbors.

3. Previous dog-owning experience will give you a good idea of what a dog

The PRT is an active companion who will enjoy all sorts of outdoor excursions. Again, safety is of the utmost importance, as it doesn't take much to pique the PRT's interest and have him off and running in no time.

expects from you and what you must do for your dog. Since the PRT is one of the more active breeds, you must be able to handle this roller-coaster of a canine companion. In addition, the PRT is smart and needs an owner that is equally as smart, or smarter, than he is! Are you up for the ride?

4. The PRT will not tolerate any mistreatment from a child. Unlike a Great Dane or Golden Retriever, who will allow a child to ride on his back or pull his ears or

Don't under-estimate the breed's ability as an escape artist when constructing a proper fence; the PRT is well versed in the arts of digging, jumping and climbing, even more so if he has a partner in crime.

tail, the PRT is an assertive breed and will demand respect. The Parson Russell Terrier Club of America does not recommend this breed for families who have children under the age of six unless the owners have experience with PRTs.

5. As a responsible dog owner, it is up to you to make certain that your dog is trained not to bark needlessly or excessively. The Parson Russell, being a bit of a know-it-all, can be a tad noisy. Once again, it is not fair to your neighbors to leave your dog outside to bark endlessly. Be consid-erate and be consistent in training your dog, and your neighbors won't despise your barky PRT.

6. Even though you will not have to groom the PRT's coat too often, you will need to trim his toenails, wash his face once or twice a week, keep his ears clean and give him baths as needed. The broken-coated PRT requires a bit more coat care than the smooth, but no PRT requires nearly as much grooming as many of the other terriers.

In spite of the toughness of the dog, the PRT is appreciated for his intelligence, his devotion to his family, his abilities for guarding those around him and their possessions and his good looks. However, do take time to learn about the breed! Do not just rush out and buy the first puppy you see.

For more information on the Parson Russell Terrier, you can research the breed and make contact with breed club members. Take a look at the breed's page on the AKC and UKC sites, and also visit the PRT Club of America's site (www.prtca.org) and/or the sites of the UKC-affiliated national PRT clubs. These websites are excellent sources of trusted information and can direct you to local PRT clubs, breeders and other experienced breed folk, all helpful sources of advice.

ARE YOU A PRT PERSON?

Overview

- Two words all prospective PRT owners should bear in mind: *hunting* and *terrier*.
- The PRT requires an intelligent and active owner who will devote himself to giving the dog the required time, training and attention.
- Before beginning the search for a PRT puppy, it is wise to study the breed, understand its personality and be sure that you have what it takes to properly raise and train this feisty, energetic and sometimes overly vocal terrier.
- Owning a PRT has been likened to a "roller-coaster ride," one that's sure to have its ups and downs but overall will be very fun-filled, rewarding and fulfilling for dog and owner.

CHAPTER 4

Selecting a PRT Breeder

When you buy your Parson Russell Terrier, you will want to buy a healthy puppy from a responsible breeder. This may sound as if we're overstating the obvious, but you would be surprised at how many people purchase puppies as "impulse buys." The purchase of a dog requires more consideration than the purchase of, say, a new leather coat, dinette set or lawn mower, yet too often people purchase puppies from unsavory sources, with no

Look for happy, well-adjusted pups who have been raised in the breeder's home as part of family life, not isolated in a kennel environment.

recommendations or without doing sufficient research. Hopefully, you are one of the smart ones, someone who is reading this book before he has a PRT puppy chewing on his shoelaces.

So what qualifies someone as a responsible breeder? A responsible breeder is a person who has given considerable thought before breeding his bitch. He considers health problems in the breed, has room in his home to properly raise puppies and has the time to devote to a swarming litter of baby PRTs. He does not breed to the dog down the block because it is convenient, and he does not have a litter to show his kids the miracle of birth with the family pet.

Further, a responsible breeder is someone who is dedicated to the breed and to breeding out any faults and hereditary problems, and whose overall interest is in improving the breed. He will study pedigrees and

Dedicated breeders have a passion for the PRT and will usually keep multiple dogs themselves. Meet these dogs so that you get a good idea of how the breeder's line matures—do they possess the characteristics that you want in your home for the next decade or probably more?

Meet at least one of the parents and assess his or her characteristics, as not only the parents' looks and health but also personality traits are passed on to the litter.

see what the leading stud dogs are producing. To find the right stud dog for his bitch, he may fly his bitch across the country to breed to a particular stud dog, or he may drive the bitch to the dog, who may be located a considerable distance away. He may have only one or two litters a year, which means that there may not be a puppy ready for you when you first call, but remember that your puppy will be a new family member and usually the wait will be well worthwhile.

If you've really found a good breeder, you will find that he has been "in the breed" for several years, has bred several litters, has bred and/or shown champions (whether at AKC or UKC dog shows, or both) and belongs to the national and regional PRT clubs. You should try to find a person who is connected in the dog world, who has references that can be checked instantly. You've hit paydirt (good for a terrier person) if your chosen breeder is someone who is known on the national level.

WHERE TO LOOK FOR A BREEDER

So now let's talk about how you go about finding such a breeder! To start, you can ask your veterinarian. If you don't have one, ask a friend's vet for a referral. Breeders usually have nice rapports with their vets (they're good customers, you know). A vet, therefore, will happily recommend someone who presents him with a litter of healthy pups. Another option is to spend the day at a dog show or an obedience trial, where you can meet breeders and handlers and get to know their dogs. Most PRT devotees are more than happy to show off their dogs and brag about their accomplishments. Also, if you know a PRT of which you are fond, ask the owner where the dog came from. Hopefully the dog came from a good breeder or a breed club's rescue scheme, as these are really your only trusted sources.

Of course, when you check out the websites of the national PRT clubs, you will find listings of their regional clubs across

WHERE *NOT* TO LOOK

Skip the puppy ads in your local newspaper. Reputable breeders rarely advertise in newspapers, because they have

Mother's milk starts the pups off in life with optimum nutrition and protection against disease. The breeder ensures that all pups nurse properly and supervises their eventual weaning.

the US. You should be able to find a club in your area of the country, likely in your state. The local club should be able to put you in touch with responsible member breeders and will also be able to answer any questions that you may have.

contacts in the dog world. Some breeders place ads in the dog magazines, which is much better than the local newspaper. Good breeders are very particular about prospective puppy owners and do not rely on mass advertising to attract the right people. Instead, they depend on referrals from other breeders and previous puppy clients. They are more than willing to keep any puppy past the usual eight-week placement age until the right person comes along. Do not purchase a puppy advertised on a sign in your local supermarket or favorite sandwich shop. Backyard breeders do not have the experience required to produce a healthy, sound litter. Don't chance your new puppy on someone's hobby or an accidental mating.

VISITING THE BREEDER

The responsible breeder happily will give you a tour of his kennel (or breeding facility) and invite you into his home to see the puppies. The areas will be clean and smell good. The breeder will show you the dam of the litter that you are considering and she will be clean, smell good and be groomed. Likewise, the

puppies will be clean, with trimmed toenails and clean faces.

Just as you have researched the breeder, be prepared for the breeder to ask you some questions. He will be interested in knowing things like the following: Have you owned a dog before? How many have you owned and have you ever owned a PRT? Did your dogs live long lives with you? Do you have a fenced yard? How many children do you have and what are their ages? Are you willing to spend the time in training your children in how to treat the new canine family member? Have you ever done any dog training and are you willing to go to obedience classes with your PRT? Are there any other pets in your household? Are you interested in showing your PRT? Do not be offended by these questions. The breeder has invested a lot of effort and money into this litter and his first priority is to place each pup in a caring and appropriate household where he will be wanted, loved and cared for.

New owners should inquire about the necessary paperwork that accompanies the puppy. For starters, ask to see the pedigree and registration papers. Although AKC or UKC registration is no guarantee of quality, it is one small step in the right direction. If you hope to show your pup or enter licensed competitions, registration with the AKC or UKC is necessary.

The pedigree should include three to five generations of ancestry. Inquire about any titles in the pedigree. Titles simply indicate a dog's accomplishments in some area of canine competition; they prove the merits of the ancestors and add to the breeder's credibility. The UKC offers Performance Pedigrees, which give more information about each dog, including how many champion offspring each ancestor produced. While it is true that,

like the registration, a pedigree cannot guarantee health or good temperament, a well-constructed pedigree is still a good insurance policy and a

This happy mom is proud to pose with her pretty pup. She and the breeder have been the litter's caregivers up to this point; are you ready to take it from here?

good starting point. There should be no extra fee, by the way, for either the pedigree or registration papers. The papers do not cost extra, and any breeder who charges for these documents is unscrupulous.

THE PURCHASE

Some breeders aren't shy about telling you that you are *purchasing* this puppy, not adopting it. While adopting sounds much nicer, this is a sales transaction and money is involved. You can expect to pay a dear price for all of the qualities of a good breeder and good puppy, whether you purchase a PRT for a companion dog or one for show or working potential. Breeders will evaluate their puppies, and those puppies with little or no show potential are considered "pet quality" and sold for less than their "show-quality" pups. "Pet quality," of course, does not mean unsound

Although a puppy will not yet conform to the specifics of the breed standard, physical soundness and typical temperament should be evident even in youngsters.

or atypical. A pet must be as healthy and sound as any top show dog, and the pet PRT should look and act like a PRT. The discount or bargain PRT is not a bargain at all. Indeed, the discount pup is in reality a potential disaster that has little chance of developing into a healthy, stable adult. Such "bargains" could ultimately cost you a fortune in vet expenses as well as heartache that can't be measured in dollars and cents.

Most reputable breeders have puppy sales contracts that include specific health guarantees and reasonable return policies. The breeder should agree to accept a puppy back if things do not work out. He also should be willing, indeed anxious, to check up on the puppy's progress after the pup leaves for his new home and be available for help and advice if you have questions or problems with the pup.

SELECTING A PRT BREEDER

Overview

- It won't be difficult to find a breeder of the popular PRT, but it will take time to find a *good* breeder, which is the only kind of breeder from whom you should obtain your pup.
- A reputable breeder's goals lie in improving the PRT and passing on only the best breed qualities from one generation to the next.
- The AKC and UKC, along with their PRT affiliate clubs, are trusted sources for breeder referrals. Check with them online or visit one of their events to make contacts in the breed.
- Remember that, as much as you are scrutinizing the breeder, he is doing the same to you in considering whether you will be a fit owner for one of his precious pups.
- Discuss documentation provided and all terms of the sale with the breeder before you agree to purchase a puppy.

CHAPTER 5

Finding the Right Puppy

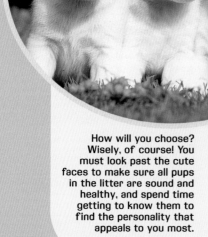

How will you choose? Wisely, of course! You must look past the cute faces to make sure all pups in the litter are sound and healthy, and spend time getting to know them to find the personality that appeals to you most.

Before visiting the litter, you should consider whether you prefer a male or a female pup. Some consider males to be easier to train but the more aggressive of the two sexes. Others prefer the softer disposition of the female. In the PRT, size will make little difference, since there will be a variance of only an inch or so between the male and female.

If you do not plan to spay or neuter your pet (and some breeders will *require* you to spay or neuter a pet-only PRT), a female will come into season approximately every six months. This can be a difficult time for up to three weeks, as it is fairly messy and will attract any loose males in the neighborhood, who will sit on your doorstep like lovelorn swains. Males who are not neutered can be more aggressive and will have more of a tendency to lift their legs and to mount whatever they can! If you are not sure which sex you want, discuss it with the breeder; he will be able to give you some direction. In addition to sex considerations, coat type may also play a role in your choice.

Your chosen pup will jump for joy in anticipation of becoming your new best friend!

Here are some general rules about selecting the right puppy from the litter. All litters are different, and all puppies are unique. Keep this in mind, as there are no rules set in granite when it comes to picking the perfect pup for you. When looking over the pups, do not pick the puppy

Look at that face! You can't take home every puppy you meet, but meeting breeders and puppies is such a fun and informative part of learning about the PRT.

that hangs back. You also should think twice before picking the most outgoing pup in the litter. However, do keep in mind that, in this breed, all puppies will be quite active and some even a bit hyper! Hyper puppies can turn into hyper adults (but not always) and will require more patience and time in training. Look for the middle-of-the-road puppy, the one that is interested, approaches you, listens when you speak and looks very alert. Never pick the pup that will not come up to you; shyness can lead to problem behavior in the future. Likewise, you should never pick a puppy because you "feel sorry" for him. You are adding a new member to your family and you want one that is bright, healthy and, of course, fun!

If this is your first puppy, understand that there will be expenses in addition to the price of the puppy. You will need to purchase the necessary accessories as well as making sure that your yard is securely fenced and escape-proof. Of course, there's the daily expense of dog food, which is by no means cheap (for a quality brand). Also, there are veterinary bills, which can be significant, especially if you're visiting frequently for treatments or for unexpected "nuisance problems" (like hot spots, ear infections, etc.). For a small breed like the PRT, the overall expenses can be less than those for a large breed. Your grooming expenses will also be less than those for a heavily coated breed that needs elaborate grooming tools and/or trips to the salon. However, the PRT does come with expenses of which you must be aware.

ADULT OPTIONS

If you think that you are not up to the challenge of raising and training a PRT puppy, you can consider the acquisition of an adult. Adopting an adult may be the perfect solution to your desire for a dog in your very busy life. First, you should consider a "rescue" PRT. This is a dog who, for any number of reasons, is in need of a new home. Such a PRT will usually be over one year of age and possibly obedience-trained and housebroken (though not necessarily). The breed rescue organization will bathe and groom the dog in addition to providing a veterinarian's health certificate attesting to the dog's good health.

Usually these dogs make marvelous pets, as they are grateful for a second chance at a loving home. Not only do the national clubs have active rescue organizations, but local clubs will also have groups of individuals working in their areas. Rescue committees consist of very dedicated individuals who care deeply about the breed and give countless hours of their time, in addition to money, to assure that each dog will have an equal chance in life.

With the PRT, do investigate the background of the dog as much as possible, as you do not want to be bring home the problems that someone else may have instilled in this particular dog. By going through a national PRT club's

PRT rescue schemes offer many wonderful adult dogs second chances at good homes. If this is a good option for you, take the family along to meet and interact with some of the dogs. You may just find the perfect match!

rescue organization, you should be assured of getting a dog that you will be able to live with happily.

Another option for acquiring an adult is to adopt a retired show or breeding dog from a reputable breeder. Perhaps the breeder may have an older dog that he wants to place in a good home. Space is always a consideration in a breeder's kennel. For some breeders, once they have put a championship on a dog, they would like to move the dog into a home where he will receive the optimum of attention. Oftentimes a breeder looks to re-home a retired show dog who has made his contribution to the breed, but whom the breeder does not want to include in a breeding program. Likewise, a breeder may be willing to sell a brood bitch after she has had a litter or two. Give this some thought, as often an older dog will be trained and considerably easier to live with.

SELECTING THE PUPPY

You arrive at the appointed time and the breeder has the puppies ready for you to meet. They should be a happy bunch, clean and groomed. Their noses will be wet, their coats will have a sheen and they will have a nice covering of flesh over their ribs. You will be ready to pick up one of these rascals and cuddle him in your arms!

Most likely, the breeder has raised the puppies in his home or in an adjoining kennel building. Either way, the pups should have had lots of inter-action with humans and be happy to meet and greet visitors. Socialization at an early age fosters sound temperament in the puppies.

You should ask the breeder if the sire and dam of the litter have had their temperaments tested. These tests are offered by the American Temperament Test Society (ATTS). Responsible breeders will be familiar with this organization and will have had their animals tested. The breeder will show you the score sheet and you can easily determine if the parents have the personalities you are seeking. In addition, this is an excellent indication that this is a responsible breeder.

Temperament testing by the ATTS is done on dogs that are at least 18 months of age; therefore puppies are not tested, but the sire and dam can be tested. The test is like a simulated walk through a park or a neighborhood where everyday situations are encountered. Neutral, friendly and threatening situations are encountered to observe the dog's reactions to the various stimuli. Problems that are noted are unprovoked aggression, panic without recovery and strong avoidance. Behavior toward strangers, reaction to auditory, visual and tactile stimuli and self-protective and aggressive behavior are watched. The dog is on a loose lead for the test, which takes about ten minutes to complete. The ATTS has not tested a large number of PRTs for temperament, but recent statistics show that, of those who have been tested, 84% have passed, which is a relatively high rate.

Some breeders will have the temperaments of their puppies tested by either a professional, their veterinarian or another dog breeder. This will find the high-energy pup and the pup

You will likely select your pup before he is old enough to leave the breeder and then pick him up at the proper age. Your pup must then adjust to life away from his canine pack.

that will be slower to respond, the pup with the independent spirit and the one that will want to follow the pack.

If the litter has been tested, the breeder will suggest which pup he thinks will be best for your family. If the litter has not been tested, you can do a few simple tests while you are sitting on the floor playing with the pups. Pat your leg or snap your finger and see which pup comes up to you first. Clap your hands and see if one of the litter shies away from you. See how they play with one another. Watch for the one that has the personality that appeals to you most, as this will probably be the puppy that you will take home. Look for the puppy that appears to be "in the middle," not overly rambunctious, overly aggressive or submissive. You want the joyful pup, not the wild one. Spend some time selecting your puppy and, if you are hesitant, tell the breeder that you would like to go home and think it over. This is a major decision, as you are adding a family member who may be with you for 10 to 15 years. Be sure you get the puppy with whom you will all be happy.

Visit with the dam and also the sire, if possible. In many cases, the sire is not on the premises, but the breeder should at least have photos, his pedigree and a resume of his characteristics and accomplishments. It is normal for some dams to be somewhat protective of their young, but overly aggressive behavior is unacceptable. PRTS are happy, outgoing critters, and it's rare to find a PRT that will shy away from a friendly overture. Temperament is inherited, and if one or both parents are aggressive or very shy, it is likely that some of the pups will inherit those traits.

HOMEWARD BOUND

You have selected the PRT that appeals to you. He is smart and friendly, ready to take on the world. By seven weeks of age, the pups should have had at least one worming and a first puppy shot. They also should have a vet's certificate verifying their good health at the time of the exam. Some breeders feel that separating the vaccines in a puppy's first shots reduces the possibility of negative reactions to the various components in the combination vaccines. Ask your breeder and your vet for their recommendations, and get a copy of the pup's vaccination record from the breeder.

As far as diet, the breeder should tell you what the pup has been eating, when and how much. It's nice if the breeder can send home a small supply of puppy food to get you started. Most breeders also give their clients a puppy "take-home" packet, which includes a copy of the health certificate, the puppy's pedigree and registration papers, copies of the parents' health clearances and the breeder's sales contract if he has one. Many supply literature on the breed and how to properly raise a PRT pup…perhaps that's where you got this book! Dedicated breeders know that the more you know, the better life ahead will be for their beloved PRT kids. You are now on your way to welcoming your new puppy into your family.

FINDING THE RIGHT PUPPY

Overview

- Preference for a particular sex and/or coat type may be a factor in your puppy selection, although these factors do not pose great differences in the PRT.
- Pick a friendly, sound puppy who is interested in you. Steer clear of the overly hyper puppy or the one who hides in a corner.
- If raising a puppy isn't for you, consider rescuing an adult PRT from a breed club's organization or adopting an older dog from a breeder.
- With a dog of any age come expenses, so be sure you can handle the financial aspect of PRT ownership.
- Temperament tests and the breeder's knowledge of the pups will help you find your perfect puppy match.
- Be sure that the breeder gives you all of the relevant documentation and paperwork that goes along with your pup.

CHAPTER 6

Welcoming the PRT

You have selected your puppy and are ready to bring your new family member home. Before welcoming your pup, you should have bought food and water bowls, a leash, a collar, an ID tag and a crate in which your puppy not only will sleep but also will spend his daytime hours when he is home alone. Your puppy will soon learn that the crate is his "second home," and he will feel safe and secure when he is in his crate. If left uncrated and alone, a bored pup can chew on the furniture, the woodwork or just about anything. Keeping him in a confined area when

Every member of the household should know how to safely handle a PRT puppy. Interactions between children and the pup should be supervised for safety and to foster the PRT's positive attitude toward young friends.

you are away keeps him safe while eliminating these problems. Several towels or a washable blanket in the crate will make him comfortable.

Nothing is safe from the mouths of teething pups, so owners must ensure that nothing unsafe is chewed or ingested by their PRTs.

If you are driving some distance to pick up your pet, take along a towel or two, a water pan and your leash and collar. Also take along some plastic baggies and a roll of paper towels in case there are any potty accidents or motion sickness.

Before bringing your puppy home, be aware that there are dangers in the household that must be eliminated. Electrical wires should be raised off the floor and hidden from view, as they are very tempting as chewable objects. Swimming pools, koi ponds and other such bodies of water can be very dangerous, so make certain that your puppy doesn't have access to them. Some barricades will be necessary to prevent accidents. Not all dogs can swim, and those with short legs or heavy bodies cannot

If your plucky pup seems a little hesitant at first, give him some time. The move to your home is a big one, and he will need to settle in before his terrier confidence fully emerges.

After puppy shopping, you must puppy-proof your house. Parson Russell Terrier pups are naturally curious critters that will investigate everything new, then seek-and-destroy just because it's fun. The message here is: never let your puppy roam your house or yard unsupervised. Scout your house indoors and out for the following hazards:

Trash Cans and Diaper Pails
These are natural puppy magnets (they know where the good smelly stuff is!).

Medication Bottles, Cleaning Materials, Roach and Rodent Poisons
Lock these up. You'll be amazed at what a determined puppy can find.

Electrical Cords
Unplug them wherever you can and make the others inaccessible. Injuries from chewed electrical cords are extremely common in young dogs.

Dental Floss, Yarn, Needles and Thread, Other Stringy Stuff
Puppies snuffling about at ground level will find and ingest the tiniest of objects and will end up in surgery. Most vets can tell you stories about the stuff they've surgically removed from puppies' guts.

Toilet Bowl Cleaners
If you have them, throw them out now. All dogs are born with "toilet sonar" and quickly discover that the water there is always cold.

Garage
Beware of antifreeze! It is extremely toxic and even a few drops will kill an adult PRT, less for a pup. Lock it and all other chemicals well out of reach. Fertilizers can also be toxic to dogs.

Socks and Underwear, Shoes and Slippers, Too
Keep them off the floor and close your closet doors. Puppies love all of these because they smell like you times ten!

climb out of the water. Watch your deck railings and make sure that your puppy cannot slip through the openings.

If you have young children in the house, they must understand that the small puppy is a living being and must be treated gently. They cannot pull his ears, pick him up roughly or drop him carelessly. A child taught about animals at an early age can become a lifelong compassionate animal lover and owner. Children who are not exposed to animals often become fearful around dogs. Owning a dog can be a valuable part of every child's youth. The PRT adores kids and will tag along beside them all day. Be a responsible, sensible parent and dog owner. Consider where a young child can get into trouble, and your puppy will be right behind him!

When puppy comes into the house for the first time (after he has relieved himself outside), let him look at his new home and surroundings, then give him a light meal and some water. When he is tired, take him for another potty trip and then tuck him into his crate either to take a nap or, better yet, to sleep through the night.

The first day or two for your puppy should be fairly quiet, giving him time to get used to his new home, surroundings and family. He may cry a bit the first night, but you can put a teddy bear or a soft, woolly sweater in his crate to give him some warmth and security. A nearby ticking clock or a radio playing soft music can also be helpful.

Remember, your pup has been uprooted from his siblings, his mother and his familiar human (the breeder), and he will need a day or two to get used to his new family. If he should cry, let him be and he will eventually quiet down and sleep. By the third night, he should be well settled in. Have patience and, within a week or less, it will seem to you, your family and your puppy that you have all been together for years.

WELCOMING THE PRT

Overview

- Have the puppy necessities in place before you bring your puppy home.
- Also before the pup comes home, you must puppy-proof your home, eliminating hazards and creating a safe, secure environment for your pup indoors and out.
- Child-pup interactions should be supervised, and children must treat the pup with care.
- Help the pup settle in. Be patient, especially during the first few nights, as he gets used to his new home and family.

House Lessons for Your PRT Puppy

Since our society hasn't yet devised a "finishing school" for puppies, dog owners continue to home-school their dogs. Some dog owners, honestly, wouldn't mind sending their irascible PRT rascals to finishing school when they are ten weeks old and then receiving the pups back when they are handsome, well-behaved six-month-olds! Nevertheless, you, as the willing owner of a PRT, will be taking on the responsibility of the socialization, housebreaking and

Enforcing some rules around the house with your PRT will be necessary to ensure that he becomes a happy, well-adjusted, well-behaved canine citizen with whom you enjoy sharing your life and home.

other general education of your new little rascal!

SOCIAL ETIQUETTE

Your PRT's social skills began in the whelping box with his dam. There he learned how to talk "dog" and how to interact in proper canine body language. What does a growl mean? What does rolling on my back mean? What does it mean when mom slicks back her ears and shows me her teeth? Likewise, your pup and his littermates learned the social rules and canine hierarchy through play...wrestling, chasing, nipping (not too hard) and licking. Your family now becomes your pup's "social circle" and must introduce him to humans (big and small) and other dogs (mostly bigger). Socializing your puppy is very important if you want a dog that fits into your home and that you are able to take out in public with no problems. A PRT who is a good

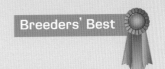

Part of training means encouraging proper chewing behavior. You don't want to deal with the aftermath of bored terrier teeth!

Once your pup is accustomed to walking politely on a traditional lead, he can graduate to a flexible lead. Your inquisitive PRT will appreciate having a wider area to explore while you will appreciate being able to safely control him on his expeditions.

companion is enjoyed by everyone.

Socializing a puppy is similar to when you bring home a new baby. A baby needs to be held, cuddled and loved, and so does your pup! Hold and pet your puppy so that he knows that he is wanted and loved. Do not play with him constantly, though, as he is very young and needs time to rest up and sleep.

Once he has had the

and let him play for a few minutes. Take him for short walks in public places where he will see people and other dogs as well as hear strange noises. Watch other dogs, however, as they are not always friendly. Keep your PRT on a short leash and you will have control over him so he does not jump on anyone.

All dogs thrive on structure and routine. Keep your PRT pup to a schedule as much as

The crate has many benefits in training your PRT and keeping him safe. Besides providing him with a secure place of his own in the home, it is an invaluable tool for house-breaking, travel safety and having a place for him to go when you cannot supervise.

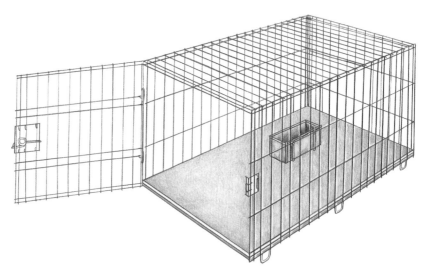

necessary vaccinations (ask your vet when it is safe for him to be out and about), let your pup meet the neighbors

you can, as he will become schedule-oriented very quickly. If he knows that you rise at 7 a.m. every day and that shortly after you will take him out, he will wait for you to let him out before relieving himself in his crate. He may even get used to your getting up at 9 a.m. on Saturdays and Sundays (but not during the first month!).

Habits, and that includes good and bad habits, that are learned at an early age become lifelong habits. Thus it goes without saying that it is best to start out on the right foot. Don't let your PRT chew on the leg of the old kitchen table and think that it's cute, because before long he will have chewed up the leg of your expensive dining room table. He won't know the difference, but you will! Likewise, don't give him your old leather shoe to gnaw on, because he may decide it's time to taste your Guccis next week. Set limits and make sure that the pup understands them, accepts them and sticks to them. Your consistency is the key to his understanding

the house rules and the daily routine.

Keep your pup confined to a specific area, such as the kitchen or den, until he is trained and fairly mature. Use baby gates and barricades and he will quickly learn that he is welcomed in certain areas of the house and not welcomed in other areas. And, of course, put him into his crate when you leave home, as he will be comfortable in his "house" and he will sleep until you return. The crate, as you will see, becomes the key element in house-training the pup.

WHO ARE YOU CALLING "JACK?"

One of the most important factors in training a young pup is to give him a name. "Jack" once was a great name for the PRT...though today it seems that owners are a bit more creative! Sometimes it may take a week or so before you find a name that fits the dog. Other times, you will have the pup named before you even bring him home. In general, short one- or two-syllable names are the easiest for the purposes of training. It's easy to say, "Heel, Nipper" or "Down, Captain." It's not so easy to say "Off, Methuselah" or "Roll over, Beethoven." You want a name that not only fits the personality of the dog but one that fits the breed itself (though it's not much easier to say "Roll over Vaughn-Williams!"). If you pick a sensible, easy name, your dog will quickly know that you are talking about him.

HOUSEBREAKING 101

Your dog must be house-broken, and this job should begin as soon as you bring him home. Diligence during the first two or three weeks will surely pay off. House-breaking a PRT should be a relatively easy task since the breed is so smart. Of course, crates are a major help in housebreaking, and most breeders wouldn't dream of housebreaking their PRTs without using crates. Crate training revolves around the principle that canines do not like to soil their dens (in this case, their crates). Thus a puppy in his crate will naturally try to keep his crate clean.

You must do your part in the crate-training process. You cannot expect a puppy to "hold it" for very long. Like toddlers, puppies have little control over their bladder and muscles, so be ready! Every time your puppy wakes up from a nap, he should be quickly put outside. Watch him and praise him with "Good boy!" when he urinates or defecates. Give him a pat on the head and take him inside. He may have a few accidents, but with the appropriate "No" from you, he will quickly learn that it is better to go outside and do his "duty" than to do it on the kitchen floor and be scolded.

You must have a dog with clean toileting habits. Training your pup to a chosen relief spot outdoors will teach him that this is the place to go when he needs "to go."

CHAPTER 7

You will soon learn the habits of your dog and you will recognize his body-language signals that indicate his need "to go." However, at the following times it is essential to take your dog out: when he gets up in the morning, after he eats, before he goes to bed, after long naps and anytime he's been released from his crate. As an adult, your PRT likely will only have to go out three or four times a day.

Some dogs will go to the door and bark when they want to be let out and others will nervously circle around. Watch and learn from his signs. Be patient with the housebreaking process, as this can sometimes be a trying time. You must stick with it, as it is simply essential to have a clean house dog. Life will be much easier for all of you—not to mention better for the carpeting!

DRIVER'S ED

You should accustom your dog to riding in the car at an early age. Most dogs love to ride and, if given the opportunity, they would gladly take the driver's seat! Teach your PRT good car manners, such as not riding on the driver's lap, no racing about the car from window to window and no chewing on the arm rests. Although your PRT will never agree, the best way for him to travel in the car is in his crate. This takes a lot of the fun out of the drive—making a wet noseprint on every window,

The half-squat? The anxious look? Learn your PRT's body language, because these cues are telling you loud and clear that it's time to get outside now!

leaping from front to back seat and back again, sleeping at a passenger's feet and barking at passing cars and dogs—but it does guarantee that you all reach your destination alive and sane.

It is very important to remember not to take your dog out in the car on a hot day and that you never leave him alone for even a few minutes in the car. A car can heat up very quickly at any time of year, and the dog will not be able to cope with the heat. Leaving the window open a crack poses a danger as well, as a panicked dog may try to escape, injuring himself in the process. Heat stroke is a very real threat to all dogs, so use your common sense and keep your PRT safe and cool.

HOUSE LESSONS FOR YOUR PRT

Overview

- The responsibility of teaching acceptable "social skills" falls on you, the PRT owner.
- Socialization, introducing the pup to other people, strange dogs, new experiences, etc., is essential to your PRT's growing up happy, confident and well-behaved in the home and out in public.
- Be consistent! Decide on the house rules, enforce them and make sure all family members stick to them.
- Pick a name for your puppy and use it often so that he learns that it refers to him.
- Your PRT must be housebroken, taught to adopt proper toileting habits, if the two of you are going to happily share a clean home.
- Consider your PRT's safety and comfort when traveling. Whether you travel with him often or just take him to the vet, he should be accustomed to riding in the car.

PRT Puppy Kindergarten

Your well-socialized puppy, integrated into your everyday life, should now be used to the family and to strangers. Household noises like the telephone, TV and vacuum cleaner, and street sounds like car horns and fire sirens, will not startle or upset him. He's adjusted nicely to your lifestyle, family and home, and wants to fit right in.

You will find it to your advantage to have a mannerly dog, one who will be welcomed when you travel to visit friends and one whom your own visitors look forward to

Your PRT is a bright and eager student, able to learn quickly. Your main challenges in training will be keeping him focused on and interested in the lesson, not the distractions around him.

seeing. To that end, learning some basic commands will make your PRT a better canine citizen. Consider having one of the family members attend puppy kindergarten classes with your pup. From these basic classes, the foundation for all future training will be laid. This two-month class is geared toward puppies from two to five months of age. You will cover the basics: sit, heel, down, stay and recall (or come). There are definite advantages to your dog's mastering each of the commands. Sit and heel are great helps when walking your dog. Who needs a puppy walking between your legs, lunging forward or lagging behind, in general acting like a nut? You want your dog to walk like a gentleman on your left side and sit as you wait to cross the street. Recall is very important if your dog escapes from the yard, breaks his leash or otherwise gets away from you

Your PRT must be accustomed to his collar, because you will teach the basics with the dog on lead.

You'll find that your PRT is more than willing to plop down whenever he needs a break, but less likely to assume the down position when someone tells him to.

and you need to call him back.

Here is a short rundown of the commands. If you attend puppy classes or obedience training classes, you will have

Place your dog on your left side as you are standing and firmly say "Sit." As you say this, run your hand down your PRT's back and gently push him into a sitting

Once proficient in the sit exercise, your dog can progress to the sit/stay. Only practice this command off-lead in a securely enclosed area, just in case "stay" isn't what your PRT has in mind.

professional help in learning these commands. However, you and your dog can learn these very basic exercises on your own.

SIT COMMAND
This is the exercise with which you should begin.

position. Praise him, hold him in this position for a few minutes, release your hand, praise him again and give him a treat. Repeat this several times a day, perhaps as many as ten times. Before long, your pup will understand what you want.

STAY COMMAND

Teach your dog to stay in a seated position until you call him. Have your dog sit and, as you say "Stay," place your hand in front of his nose and take a step or two, no more at the beginning, away. After ten seconds or so, call your dog. If he gets up before the end of the command, have him sit again and repeat the stay command. When he stays until called (remembering to start with a very short period of time), praise him and give him a treat. As he learns this command, increase the space that you move away from the dog as well as the length of time that he stays.

HEEL COMMAND

Have your dog on your left side, with his leash on, and teach him to walk with you. If your pup lunges forward, give the leash a quick snap and say a firm "No." Then continue to walk your pup, praising him as he walks nicely by your side. Again, if he lunges, snap his leash quickly and say a smart "No." He will quickly learn that it is easier and more pleasant to walk by your side. Never allow him to lunge at someone passing by the two of you.

COME COMMAND

This command has life-saving potential...preventing your PRT from running into the street, going after a squirrel,

In the beginning of teaching the sit, the dog may need a gentle push on his rump to show him the correct position.

chasing a child on a bike, the list goes on and on.

Always practice this command on leash. You can't

afford to risk failure, or your pup will learn that he does not have to come when called. Once you have the pup's attention, call him from a short distance with "Puppy, Come!" (use your happy voice!) and give a treat when he comes to you. If he hesitates, tug him to you gently with his leash. Grasp and hold his collar with one hand as you dispense the treat. This is important. You will eventually phase out the treat and switch to hands-on praise only. This maneuver also connects holding his collar with coming and treating, which will assist you in countless future behaviors. Do 10 or 12 repetitions 2 or 3 times a day. Once pup has mastered the come command, continue to practice daily to engrave this most important behavior into his tiny brain. Experienced PRT owners know, however, that you can never completely trust a dog to come when called if the dog

The use of ample praise, gentle encouragement and, of course, tasty tidbits goes a long way in convincing the dog that he will be at ease in the down position, which is a submissive posture for dogs and thus not a favorite.

is bent on a self-appointed mission. "Off-leash" is often synonymous with "out of control."

legs out into the down position. A treat in your right hand will coax him to follow your hand into the down

This puppy just can't wait to learn to heel! Your PRT needs daily walks, so heeling is essential if you want your excursions to be enjoyable for both of you.

DOWN COMMAND

This will probably be the most complicated of the five basic commands to teach. Place your dog in the sit position, kneel down next to him and place your right hand under his front legs and your left hand on his shoulders. As you say "Down," gently push his front

position. Once you have him down, talk gently to him, stroke his back so that he will be comfortable and then praise him and give him the treat.

OTHER HELPFUL COMMANDS

There are some commands, not taught in obedience

classes, that you and your PRT will learn on your own. "Off" is an important command, as a PRT will become active and agile enough to finish off the candy dish on the coffee table or jump up onto the kitchen table for the butter. Tell him "Off, Sport" and then push him down on his four feet. Again, dogs are smart, particu-

larly PRTs, and he will quickly learn what "Off" means, whether he likes it or not.

Another good command is "Kennel up" or "Crate time," a command to tell the dog that it's time to go to his crate. Along with "Kennel up," you will teach "Bedtime" when it's time to go to his crate for the night. Do not confuse the two. Your PRT will quickly learn that "Bedtime" means a treat and then to bed for the night and that "Kennel up" or "Crate time" means that you are going out and will be back in a few hours.

Of course, the most basic of commands, which is learned very quickly, is "No." Say it firmly and with conviction every time. Again, your dog will learn that this means to keep off, don't do it or don't even think about it!

TRAINING TIPS

In all of your commands, you must be fair (don't tell him to sit when he is already

"Off" will be a helpful command in many situations. Of course, it's up to you whether or not your dog is allowed on the furniture, but you will need to be consistent with "Off" if you decide not to share your couch with your PRT.

sitting), you must be consistent (don't let him jump up onto the sofa sometimes and not at other times) and you must be firm in voicing your commands, using the same words each time. After the dog does what you want, give him a pat on the head and praise: "Good boy, Sport!" If he has achieved some great success, give him a treat along with the praise. Always praise for correct behavior!

A big part of training is patience, persistence and routine. Teach each command the same way every time. Do not lose your patience with the dog, as he will not understand what you are doing. Reward him for performing his command properly. With a PRT, you will find that your puppy will learn these commands very quickly. Your friends, when they come to your house for a dinner party, will also appreciate a well-behaved dog who will not jump on their clothing or land in their laps while they are having cocktails.

PRT PUPPY KINDERGARTEN

Overview

- Along with being socialized, your PRT needs an education in the basic commands to become a mannerly canine citizen.
- The basic commands include sit, stay, heel, come and down.
- Consider enrolling in a puppy kindergarten class to help both of you learn the basic commands.
- Beyond the basics, there are helpful commands like "Off," "Crate time" and, of course, "No," which will help you enforce the house rules.
- Be patient and be consistent with your dog's training, always rewarding him for correct behavior with verbal praise, petting and sometimes a treat.

CHAPTER 9

Home Care for Your PRT

Every home with a pet should have a first-aid kit. You can acquire all of these items at one time but more likely you will add them to your kit as you need them. You should keep all of your first-aid items together in a box, kept in a place where you can reach it quickly. Here are the items you will need:

• Alcohol for cleaning a wound;

• Antibiotic salve for treating the wound;

• Over-the-counter eye wash in case

This PRT is ready with his home health-care kit; are you?

your dog gets something in his eyes or just needs to have his eyes cleaned—"to get the red out";

- Forceps for pulling out wood ticks, thorns and burs;
- Styptic powder for when a toenail has been trimmed too short and bleeds;
- Rectal thermometer;
- A nylon stocking to be used as a muzzle if your pet should be badly injured.

Weight control is an important issue for dogs of all breeds. The PRT should be in trim condition, looking agile and muscular like this fit fellow.

Many of these items can be purchased very reasonably from your local drug store, and some you may already have in stock as household items.

Once your PRT is mature and remaining well, he will only need a yearly visit to the veterinary clinic for a check-up and a booster shot for vaccines. At these visits, the vet will also thoroughly check the dog's teeth and possibly perform a dental scraping. You may also want the vet

Get in the habit of checking your PRT's eyes and ears regularly, and make cleaning them part of your grooming routine.

to check and express the dog's anal glands if needed.

You may purchase a dental tool and clean your PRT's teeth yourself. Set the dog on the grooming table, with his head secured, and gently scrape away any tartar. Some animals will let you do this, and others will not, so you may just want to leave this to the vet. Regular toothbrushing and a crunchy dog treat every night before bedtime will help to keep the tartar down.

Expressing the anal glands is not the greatest of tasks, besides being quite smelly, so you may find that it is easier to have this done during the yearly trip to the vet's clinic. On occasion, the anal glands will become impacted, requiring veterinary assistance to clean them out.

By now you know your dog well, you know how much he eats and sleeps and how hard he plays. As with all of us, on occasion he may "go off his feed" or appear to be sick. If he has been nauseated for 24 to 36 hours, or has had diarrhea for the same amount of time, or has drunk excessive water for five or six days, a trip to the veterinarian is in order. Make your appointment and tell the receptionist why you need the appointment right away!

The veterinarian will ask you the following questions:
• When did he last eat a normal meal?
• How long has he had diarrhea or been vomiting?
• Has he eaten anything in the last 24 hours?
• Could he have eaten a toy or a piece of clothing or anything else unusual?
• Is he drinking more water than usual?

The veterinarian will check your dog over from head to tail, take his temperature and pulse, listen to his heart, feel his stomach for any lumps, look at his gums and teeth for color and check his eyes and ears. He will probably also

The PRT loves to spend time outdoors, but there are critters out there who love to spend time on dogs! Aside from the common parasites, watch out for bee stings, insect bites and allergies, and be sure the outdoor areas to which your dog has access are free of chemicals and fertilizers.

draw blood to run tests.

At the end of the examination, the vet will decide how to proceed. He may send your dog home with you with some antibiotics, he may take some x-rays or he may keep the dog overnight for observation. Follow your veterinarian's instructions and you will find that very often your dog will be back to normal in a day or two. In the meantime, feed him light meals and keep him quiet, perhaps confined to his crate.

Parasites can be a problem and there are certain ones of

This greatly enlarged flea gives you an up-close-and-personal look at this menace to dog society.

which you should be aware. Heartworm can be a deadly problem; some parts of the country can be more prone to this than others, as heart-

worms are transmitted through mosquito bites. Heartworms become very massive and wrap themselves around the dog's heart. If not treated, the dog will eventually die.

In the spring, call your veterinarian and ask if your dog should have a heartworm test. If so, take him to the clinic and the vet will give your dog a test to make certain that he is clear of heartworm. He then will be put on heartworm medication. This is important, particularly if you live in an area where mosquitoes are present.

Fleas are also a problem that can be found most anywhere, but particularly in the warmer parts of the country. You can purchase flea powder or a collar or ask your veterinarian what he recommends, such as a "spot on" treatment to kill fleas and ticks. If you suspect the presence of fleas, lay your dog on his side, separate the coat to the skin and see if you see any skipping, jumping or skittering around of little bugs.

Ticks are more prevalent in areas where there are tall grasses, shrubs and trees. Ticks are small (to start) and dark and they like to attach themselves to the warm parts of the ears, the leg pits, face folds, etc. The longer they stay on the dog, the bigger they become, filling themselves with your pet's blood and becoming as big as a dime. Take your forceps and carefully pull the tick out to make sure you get the pincers. Promptly flush the tick down the toilet or light a match to it. Put alcohol on the wound and a dab of antibiotic salve. Check your PRT often for ticks.

Let common sense and a good veterinarian be your guide in coping with these and other health problems. The more you know about your dog's health and the better you know your dog, the better you can care for your PRT.

HOME CARE FOR YOUR PRT

Overview

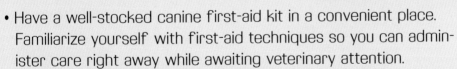

- Have a well-stocked canine first-aid kit in a convenient place. Familiarize yourself with first-aid techniques so you can administer care right away while awaiting veterinary attention.
- Your adult dog will see the vet annually for a thorough checkup and booster shots, but you are in charge of his health care every day at home.
- Since you know your dog well, you will know when something's not right, a signal to make an appointment with the vet right away.
- Discuss with your vet the safest and best way to protect your dog from parasites, from the pesky to the potentially deadly.

Feeding Your Parson Russell Terrier

To keep your Parson Russell Terrier in tip-top shape, you should feed him a quality food that is appropriate for his age and lifestyle. The premium dog-food manufacturers have developed their formulas with strict controls, using only quality ingredients obtained from reliable sources. Only a top-quality food will provide the proper balance of the vitamins, minerals and fatty acids that are

Your PRT needs a good-quality food designed to meet his needs based on age, size and activity level. Manufacturers make specific formulas to meet these criteria for different types of dogs.

necessary to support healthy bone and muscle, skin and coat.

CHOW TIME FOR PUPPY

Nutrition for your puppy is actually very easy. Dog-food companies hire many scientists and spend millions of dollars on research to determine what will be a healthy diet for your dog at all stages of life. Your breeder should have weaned the pups onto a

"Make room for me!" The breeder starts the litter on good-quality puppy food to wean them from their mother.

premium puppy food and you should continue on with the same brand. As the dog matures, you will change over to the adult formula of the same dog-food brand.

The labels on the food containers tell you what products are in the food (beef, chicken, corn, etc.), and list ingredients in descending order of weight or amount in the food. Do not add vitamins or anything else unless your veterinarian suggests that you do so. Do not think that by cooking up a special diet you will turn out a

Your PRT will not need very large bowls, but he will need sturdy, chew-resistant bowls that are easy to keep clean.

product that will be more nutritional than what the dog-food companies are providing. The major dog-food brands now offer foods for every breed size, age and activity level. As with human infants, puppies require a diet different from that of an adult canine. The new growth formulas contain protein and fat levels that are appropriate for proper growth in the different-sized breeds.

Your young puppy will probably be fed three times a day and perhaps as often as four times a day. As he starts growing, you will divide his daily food portion into two meals a day, one in the morning and one in the evening. By the time he reaches eight months of age, you will be changing over to the adult-formula dog food. You can check the dog-food container for the amount, per pound of weight, that you should be feeding your

dog to determine how much food he should get each day.

If feeding a dry kibble, you will add water to moisten it and possibly a tablespoon or so of a canned brand of dog food for flavor. Avoid offering "people food" tidbits, as these can cause stomach upset. In fact, certain foods, like chocolate, onions, grapes and nuts, are toxic to dogs. Choose healthy dog treats and use them judiciously; for example, give him a treat at bedtime. Keep a good covering of flesh over his ribs, but do not let your dog become a fat boy! However, the more active the dog, the more calories he will need.

Always have fresh clean drinking water available. This may include a bowl of water in the kitchen and another bowl in the yard for when he is spending time exercising and playing with you outdoors.

Feeding Your Parson Russell Terrier

Breeders' Best

If your child is responsible for your PRT's food and water, be sure that the youngster is reliable and sticks to the routine. Likewise, be sure the PRT is well behaved at mealtimes.

69

A QUESTION OF WHEN

On the subject of when to serve meals, most owners agree that scheduled meals are preferable to free-feeding (that is, leaving the bowl out all day). Scheduled meals give you one more opportunity to remind your PRT that all good things in life come from you—his master and chef. With scheduled meals, it's also easier to predict elimination, which is the better road to house-training. Regular meals help you know just how much your puppy eats and when, which is valuable information for weight control and if your pup gets sick. Most often free-feeding fosters picky eating habits...a bite here, a nibble there. Free-feeders are also more likely to become possessive of their food bowls, a problem behavior that signals the beginning of aggression.

DECISIONS FOR THE ADULT DIET

Should you feed canned or dry food? Should you offer the dry food with or without water added? Dry food is recommended by most vets, since the dry particles help clean the dog's teeth of plaque and tartar. Adding water to dry food is optional. The food hog who almost inhales his food may do better with a splash of water in his food bowl. A bit of water added immediately before eating is also thought to enhance the flavor of the food, while still preserving the dental benefits. Whether feeding wet or dry, always have drinking water available to your Parson Russell Terrier at all times.

Like people, dogs have different appetites; some will lick their food bowls clean and beg for more, while others pick at their food and leave some of it untouched. It's easy to

The breeder should be knowledgeable about the optimum diet for the PRT. She starts the pups off right and will advise new owners how best to continue.

overfeed a "chow hound." Be strong and stay the right course. Chubby puppies may be cute and cuddly, but extra weight will stress their growing joints and is thought to be a factor in the development of hip and elbow disease. Overweight pups also tend to grow into overweight adults who tire easily and will be more susceptible to other health problems. Consult your breeder and your vet for advice on how to adjust meal portions as your puppy grows.

Always remember that lean is healthy, fat is not. Research has proven that obesity is a major canine killer. Quite simply, a lean dog lives longer than one who is overweight. And that doesn't even reflect the better quality of life for the lean dog that can run, jump and play without the burden of an extra 7 or 8 pounds.

A proper diet is essential to keeping your PRT at his peak performance level, whether competing, working or just being his normal active self.

To check your dog's figure, you should be able to see a "waistline" when viewing your dog from above and see a "tuck-up" in the abdominal area when viewing him from the side. On a dog as small as the Parson Russell Terrier, 7 or 8 pounds is an enormous amount of weight. Think about it in terms of the percentage of the dog's correct weight. A bitch in good condition may weight 14 pounds. An additional 7 pounds on a Parson Russell Terrier equates to the difference between a human's weighing 120 pounds or 180 pounds. For you, that would mean it's time to cut back on the snacks, eat a reduced-calorie diet and join the gym. And your dog should lose some weight, too!

FEEDING YOUR PARSON RUSSELL TERRIER

Overview

- Dog-food companies put much research into developing complete and balanced nutrition for dogs, with specific formulas for the different life stages and different-sized breeds.
- As your PRT pup matures, his number of daily meals will be decreased and he can be switched to an adult food around eight months of age.
- Scheduled mealtimes offer many benefits as opposed to a free-feeding method.
- For maintaining the adult PRT in good condition, it is simply necessary to pick a good adult-formula dog food, appropriate for the breed's size and the individual dog's activity level, and to watch his weight so that he does not become obese.

Grooming Your PRT

D o understand before purchasing your dog that this is a breed with a coat that needs maintenance, whether you have a dog for the show ring or one that is a household pet. The Parson Russell Terrier is by no means a high-maintenance breed in terms of grooming, but think of his coat care in terms of your child—you bathe your youngster, comb his hair and put a clean set of clothes on him. The end product is that you have a child that smells and looks clean, and whom you enjoy having in your company. It is the same with your

Smooth-coated PRTs do not require much coat care other than regular once-overs with a brush or grooming glove to remove dead hair and debris and to give the coat a healthy shine.

dog—keep the dog brushed, cleaned and trimmed, and you will find it a pleasure to be in his company. However, it will require commitment to a regular grooming routine to achieve this.

The Parson Russell Terrier can have either a smooth coat, a broken coat or a rough coat. Since the PRT has a double coat, regardless of length, the coat will shed and therefore require some maintenance. Of course, the smooth coat is easier to keep up than the rough or broken coat.

The broken-coated PRT needs a little more attention to grooming, as the coat is plucked or stripped, like the coats of many terrier breeds, to stay in proper condition and texture.

For those with a smooth-coated Parson Russell, grooming will consist primarily of a weekly "go-over." Brush him down with a bristle brush or glove. Take a damp washcloth and wipe down his entire body. Once a month or so, you may want to put him in the laundry tub for a bath. You will find that this will loosen any dead coat, so after the bath be sure to

Dogs do not need to be bathed too frequently, as over-bathing can dry the skin and coat. A particularly dirty outing may require an additional bath or at least a thorough wipe-down.

brush him out thoroughly to clean out any dead undercoat. After the dog is bathed will be a good time to trim his toenails, as they will be soft and easier to trim. You may want to trim his whiskers to the skin, as this will give the dog a neat, clean-cut look. Wipe him dry with a towel or use a hair dryer on a low heat setting. If it is a nice warm, sunny day, you may want to put him out on the deck to dry (away from dirt and mud!).

If you have a rough- or broken-coated PRT, coat care for the pet can be much different and easier than that for a show dog. The vast majority of PRT fanciers own their dogs as pets and should not expect to maintain their PRTs in show coats. If you are planning to show your PRT, you will be ahead of the game if you purchase your puppy from a reputable breeder who grooms and shows his dogs. If so, this is the individual to see

for grooming lessons to learn how to get your dog ready for the show ring. Rough and broken coats need to be hand-stripped for the show ring, and this is an art that cannot be learned in a few months. Furthermore, it is very difficult (but not impossible) to learn it from a book.

If the rough or broken coat is not stripped, it will become very shaggy and the dog will not present the correct smartness that you will want to see. Again, pet grooming is different from grooming for the show ring, as you can use scissors or a clipper for trimming the pet's body and furnishings. You will have a neat, clean and trimmed dog that will still look like a Parson Russell Terrier, but he will not have the harsh coat required for the show ring. Even those with kennels who are active in the show ring will clip their old dogs or those who are no longer being shown.

Before you start grooming your PRT, be sure that you have the right surface to place the dog upon. The best option is a grooming table, available from a pet-supply shop. This should be sturdy, with a rubber mat covering the top, plus a grooming arm or "hanger." Your dog will now be comfortable even if confined and you will be able to work comfortably on the dog. Grooming can be a difficult and back-breaking job if you try to groom without a table and a grooming arm.

For the actual grooming, you will need a good-quality metal comb (with medium-spaced teeth), a slicker brush, a good sharp pair of scissors and a toenail trimmer. You may also want to purchase a flea comb (similar to the metal comb, with closer-set, thinner teeth).

Set your dog on the table and put the leash around his neck. Have the leash up behind his ears and have the leash taut when you fasten it to the eye hook on the grooming arm. Do not walk away and leave your dog unattended, as he can jump off the table and be left dangling from the leash with his feet scrambling around in the air.

Take your slicker brush and brush out the entire coat. Brush the whiskers toward the nose, the body hair toward the tail and the tail up toward the tip of the tail. Brush the leg furnishings up toward the body and brush the chest hair down toward the table. Hold the dog up by his front legs and gently

The necessary grooming equipment will vary according to your PRT's coat type. Your pet-supply store should have a wide selection from which to choose, and your breeder will be a good source of advice about which items work well.

brush the stomach hair, first toward the head and then back toward the rear. For cleanliness, you may want to take your scissors and trim the area around the penis. (or, with the girls, around the vulva).

Now that your dog is brushed out, comb through the coat with your metal comb. By now you will have removed a fair amount of dead hair and your dog will already be looking better. You may find some small mats, and these can be worked out with your fingers or your comb. If you brush your dog out every week or so, you will not have too much of a problem with mats.

For hand-stripping, you can take your dog to a professional groomer for his first couple of grooming sessions. The groomer will "set" the pattern and then it will be easier for you to get the PRT look by following the pattern that has already been set in the coat. If the coat totally grows out before you start to groom, the pattern will be lost and then you will have to start over again. Of course, you can eliminate all of the grooming for yourself, except for the weekly brushing, if you take your dog to the groomer every three months!

It is important to trim your dog's toenails, and it is best to start this within a week of bringing him home. Purchase a quality toenail trimmer for dogs. You may want to also purchase a styptic stick in case you trim the nail too short and bleeding starts. If your PRT's toenails are light in color, you will easily see the blood vessel (the "quick") that runs inside the nail. However, it is a bit more difficult to see in dark-nailed dogs and you may nick the blood vessel until you are more familiar with trimming the nails. If you do not start trimming the nails at a young age, so that your PRT is used to this, you will have greater difficulty in trimming the nails as the dog becomes larger, heavier and more difficult to hold.

If you give your dog treats of hard dog biscuits to chew on, he should not have a plaque problem. It is advisable to use a canine-formulated toothpaste and a doggie toothbrush for once-weekly toothbrushings in between veterinary visits.

For his overall health and handsome looks, give your PRT at least a weekly brushing, trim his toenails every month or so and wipe him down with a damp cloth when he looks like he needs it. Give him a bath only when it is necessary and keep his teeth clean. The result: a good-looking, well-maintained dog that you are proud to be seen with and that's in good condition!!

GROOMING YOUR PRT

Overview

- The amount of time you spend grooming will depend on your PRT's coat type, with the smooth coat being the easiest coat to care for.
- A PRT needs regular brushing, toenail trimming and bathing as needed. Too-frequent bathing is neither recommended nor beneficial.
- Grooming your rough- or broken-coated PRT will differ depending on whether he is a pet or show dog. Show dogs need to be hand-stripped to maintain proper coat texture.
- A grooming table is a wise investment, as it makes grooming easier and more comfortable for both you and your PRT.
- Nail trimming should begin in puppyhood so that your PRT tolerates the procedure.
- Make weekly toothbrushing a part of your grooming routine.

Keeping Your PRT Active

As a PRT owner, you will be amazed at your dog's athletic ability and amazing feats...especially when there's a treat involved!

Most owners of PRTs will not be wondering how to keep their dogs active; instead, they will be looking for ways to keep their dogs from bouncing off the walls. Yes, this is an active, busy breed. PRTs will keep themselves busy for hours, playing with balls or bones... or your sandals.

Your goal as a PRT owner is to find something challenging for your dog, an activity that will give him a way to harness all of his energy and talent. PRTs can excel in many activities because of their intelligence and natural agility. After puppy kindergarten, you may want to work toward a Canine Good Citizen® certificate. This is an AKC-sponsored program that, when successfully completed, shows that your dog is a well-behaved dog who reliably minds his manners at home, in public places and with other dogs. This class, available to dogs (pure-bred and otherwise) of any age, is a fun course and useful for everyday life. There are ten steps, including accepting a friendly stranger, sitting politely for petting, accepting light grooming and examination from a stranger, walking on a loose lead, coming when called, responding calmly to another dog, responding to distractions, down on command and remaining calm when the owner is out of sight for three minutes. Upon successful completion,

PRTs with their own back yards will keep themselves active on "patrol" duty, ever alert to the goings-on of the neighborhood.

Puppies love outdoor time spent in the safety of a fenced yard. Young dogs will exercise themselves just by following their noses.

your PRT will receive an AKC Canine Good Citizen® certificate.

With young pups, you will find that they like to play games of tug with hard rubber toys or knotted-up rope toys. All puppies like to chase balls and return them to their owners.

Obedience is a long-established sport at which PRTs excel. Obedience trials are held either by themselves or in conjunction with a conformation show. There are different difficulty levels. In AKC obedience, for example, the first level is Novice, whereupon completion of three passing "legs," the dog will earn a Companion Dog (CD) title. Open is the second level and the dog earns a Companion Dog Excellent (CDX) title upon completion of three successful legs. The next class is Utility (UD), which includes off-lead work, silent hand signals and picking the right dumbbells from a group

of dumbbells. Not many dogs reach this level, and it is a major accomplishment for both owner and dog when a Utility degree is achieved. The UKC offers three obedience titles similar to those of the AKC, the U-CD, U-CDX and the U-UD.

Agility is a newer sport that can be easily found at dog shows. Look for the large, noisy ring filled with competitors and dogs running the course, with excited spectators watching at ringside joining in with cheers.

In agility, dogs are taught to run a course that includes hurdles, ladders, jumps and a variety of challenges. There are a number of degrees in agility depending upon the obstacles that the dog is able to conquer. AKC defines agility as "The enjoyment of bringing together communication, training, timing, accuracy and just plain fun in the ultimate game for you and your dog."

Conformation showing is popular among dogs and fanciers of all breeds.

The UKC has adopted the agility-trial program from the North American Agility Dog Council, which awards titles in six different classes: regular, tunnelers, jumpers, weavers, gamblers and Touch N Go. No matter where your dog competes in agility, you are guaranteed lots of exercise and fun for both you and your PRT.

Earthdog trials, sponsored by the AKC, will be ideal for your PRT, since the breed was developed to go to ground. There are four class levels: Introduction to Quarry, Junior Earthdog, Senior Earthdog and Master Earthdog. Check with your local terrier clubs or Dachshund clubs to see if they offer earthdog trials. This is another challenging sport for dog and master. The UKC offers the Earth Work Hunting Program, designed to assess a terrier's ability in the field. Unlike the AKC's trials, the UKC's are not competitive, and the judge accompanies the dog to evaluate the dog's hunting ability.

For the extra-energetic PRT and owner, consider flyball! Fast, furious and fun, flyball challenges the dog's skill at catching, jumping, retrieving, running and much more. You can find out more about this fun sport by contacting the North American Flyball Association (www.flyball.org).

The ultimate in titles is the Versatile Companion Dog. This is the degree that recognizes those dogs and handlers who have been successful in multiple dog sports. In order to excel at any of these activities, it is essential to belong to a club with equipment and facilities for practice. Find a good training school in your area and attend a class as a spectator before enrolling. If you like the facility, the instructor and the type of instruction, sign your dog up for the next series of lessons.

Canine sports have become so popular with the public that

you should have little difficulty in finding a training facility. You will find it a great experience, working with your dog and meeting new people with whom you will have a common interest. This will all take time and interest on your part and a willing dog working on the other end of the leash.

Of course, the easiest way to keep your dog active and fit is to take him for walks every morning and evening. This will be good for you, too! Playing games with your dog will delight him. Retrieving games and games with his toys are always great fun for a dog. Never give him a toy or ball that is small enough for him to swallow, as this could pose a danger and end up requiring surgery to remove.

Do remember that the Parson Russell Terrier is a high-energy dog who will need lots of activities to keep him a happy camper. Don't expect him to sit around and spend his evenings watching television, as he will much prefer to be working with you in an agility class, an obedience class or just going for a nice long walk.

KEEPING YOUR PRT ACTIVE

Overview

- It's not hard to keep a PRT active, as they do pretty well on their own!
- PRTs benefit from having their energies directed in specific ways, such as the challenges of training for and competing in canine competition. They are capable of excelling at many sports.
- Canine Good Citizen®, obedience, agility, flyball and earthdog work are all worthwhile and enjoyable pursuits for the active, well-trained PRT.
- Your PRT's favorite way to stay active is by doing things with his favorite person, you!

CHAPTER 13

Your PRT and His Veterinarian

One of the things to do before bringing your PRT home is to find a good veterinarian in your area. Your breeder, if he's from your area, should be able to recommend someone; otherwise, it will be your job to find a clinic and vet that you like. You also can ask for recommendations from your dog-owning friends.

In selecting a good veterinarian, you will want to find someone, for convenience, who is within ten miles of your home. Find a veterinarian whom you like and trust, and be confident that the vet knows

It's Parson Russell, not Doctor Russell! As much as he'd like to, your PRT can't take care of his own health. Your dog's health care is a responsibility to which you commit when you decide to own a dog.

what he is doing. First impressions mean a lot when meeting your puppy's vet. See that the office looks and smells clean. It is your right to check on fees before setting up an appointment, and you will usually need an appointment. If you have a satisfactory visit, take the vet's business card so that you have all of the contact information that you need. If you are going to a clinic with a number of veterinarians in the same facility, be sure to keep track of who sees your dog. It's best to see the same vet at each visit, as he will know the history of your dog and your dog will be familiar with him.

Inquire whether the clinic takes emergency calls and, if they do not, as many no longer do, get the name, address and telephone number of the emergency veterinary service in your area and keep this handy along with your veterinarian's phone number.

On your first visit, take along the

Obvious signs of good health include bright, clear eyes and a moist (but not runny) nose.

A healthy PRT looks clean, alert and in overall good condition.

CHAPTER 13

health records that your breeder gave you with your puppy and a record of the shots that your puppy has had so that the veterinarian will know which series of shots your pup should be getting. You should also take in a fecal sample for a worm test.

VACCINATIONS

The vaccines recommended by the American Veterinary Medical Association (AVMA) are called CORE vaccines, those that protect against the diseases most dangerous to your puppy and adult dog. These include distemper (canine distemper virus, CDV), fatal in puppies; canine parvovirus (CPV or parvo), highly contagious and also fatal in puppies and at-risk dogs; canine adenovirus (CAV2), highly contagious and high risk for pups under 16 weeks of age; canine hepatitis (CA1), highly contagious, pups at high risk. These are generally combined into what

is often called a five-way shot. Rabies immunization is required in all 50 states, with the vaccine given three weeks after the complete series of the puppy shots.

Non-CORE vaccines no longer routinely recommended by the AVMA, except when the risk is present, are canine parainfluenza, leptospirosis, canine coronavirus, Bordetella (canine cough) and Lyme disease borreliosis). Your veterinarian will alert you if there are occurrences of these non-fatal diseases in your area so you can immunize your pup accordingly.

Fortunately, vaccines have kept these diseases away from our dogs, but it helps to understand each of the major canine diseases. Distemper, at one time, was the scourge of dog breeding, but with the proper immunization and a clean puppy-rearing area, this no longer presents a problem to the reputable breeder.

Canine hepatitis, very rare in the United States, is a severe liver infection caused by a virus. Leptospirosis is an uncommon disease that affects the kidneys and is rare in young puppies, occurring primarily in adult dogs. Parvovirus, recognized by fever, vomiting and diarrhea, is a deadly disease for pups and can spread very easily through their feces.

The current American Animal Hospital Association (AAHA) guidelines recommend vaccinating adult dogs every three years instead of annually. Research suggests that annual vaccinations may actually be over-vaccinating and may be responsible for many of today's canine health problems. Mindful of that, the revised AAHA guidelines on vaccinations also strongly suggest that veterinarians and owners consider a dog's individual needs and exposure before they decide on a vaccine protocol. Many

dog owners now have annual titer tests done to check their dogs' antibodies rather than automatically vaccinating for parvo or distemper.

Discuss your pup's vaccination program with your vet and decide on the safest schedule for administering his shots.

HEALTH CONCERNS IN THE PRT

The Parson Russell Terrier is, overall, a very healthy breed, but there are a few problems within the breed of which owners and prospective owners should be aware.

Lens luxation appears to

be the primary hereditary problem in the PRT. Lens luxation is a rupture of zonular attachments between the lens and the ciliary body. Lens luxation is treated by surgical extraction; vision can usually be saved if the condition is treated promptly. Left untreated, lens luxation can lead to loss of vision.

Another disorder that can occur in the Parson Russell is Legg-Calve-Perthes disease (sometimes just called Perthes). This is a bone-related disease; it is not a hereditary condition and is thought to be caused by an injury or possibly a nutritional problem. The disease appears between four and ten months of age and is very painful. An affected dog will limp on one or both rear legs and eventually the leg muscles become wasted. There are some treatments for Perthes, which should be discussed with your vet.

Some PRTs can develop hereditary cataracts. A cataract is an opacity of any size in the lens of the eye, usually milky in color and either covering the whole lens or a partial area of the lens. Congenital cataracts usually do not lead to blindness. Surgical removal is very successful, and vision will return to nearly normal when a clear plastic intraocular lens is placed in the eye.

Patellar luxation (or slipped kneecaps), once common in the breed, is less common at the present time. As breeders became aware of the problem, they made a concerted effort to breed out the problem and have met with some success.

Health guarantees are important and a responsible breeder will give you a contract that guarantees your pup against certain congenital defects. This guarantee will be limited in time to six months or one year. If there is a problem, the breeder will likely replace the pup or offer some refund of the purchase price.

TAKING GOOD CARE

In addition to hereditary problems, there is the usual "housekeeping" with your new puppy. When your dog is a young pup, you should start getting him used to an examination routine. Each time he is groomed, you should check over his ears, eyes and teeth.

Ears should be checked for dirt or any sign of infection. Take a damp cloth (a soft old washcloth can work quite well) and gently wash the inside of the ear. If you notice any buildup of wax, or a putrid smell, you should take your dog to the veterinarian to have the ears properly cleaned. If there is an infection, the vet will prescribe an ointment or liquid to clear up the problem. Dogs with upright ears have more of a chance of getting dirt into the ears whereas dogs with drop ears

have "warm" ears in which infections can grow more easily.

If you see your dog shaking his head from side to side, holding his head in an awkward position or pushing

Care of those terrier teeth is essential throughout your PRT's life, so accustom your PRT to having his mouth examined in puppyhood.

his head and ears along the side of the furniture, you can be almost certain that an ear infection is in the making.

When grooming, take your damp washcloth and gently wash the eyes. Some breeds that have excessive folds around the eyes and nostrils can have a buildup of matter that should be washed out on a daily basis with a damp tissue or cloth. Although this is not your PRT, he still can have buildup of dirt or matter around the eyes. All dogs should have their eyes checked if any redness appears. Quite often you can purchase an over-the-counter medication at the pet shop and clear up the redness. If an eye problem persists, however, you will have to see your veterinarian.

Teeth should also be checked on a regular basis. You can clean your dog's teeth yourself by using a washcloth or a piece of gauze wrapped around your finger. Gently rub your finger back and forth across the teeth as you would a toothbrush. Do not use human toothpaste, but you will find "doggy" toothpaste available if you wish to use it. If you allow plaque to build up, your dog will have as many dental problems as you would have.

Veterinarians will clean your dog's teeth, but it is a costly process and does not need to be done by a professional other than at your PRT's annual checkup if you have done your work. Giving your dog several dog biscuits a day, plus his dry kibble, will help prevent the buildup of plaque. As a dog ages, as in humans, his gums may recede, causing further problems and very smelly breath. Your vet may tell you that it is necessary to remove one or more teeth, but most dogs continue to eat well even if all of their teeth have been pulled! Of course, their diet will be a bit different, but they will fare just as well. A distinct unpleasant odor from the mouth is a signal that all is not well with your dog's gums or teeth.

All dogs have anal sacs located on either side of the rectum. The contents, very smelly, are used to mark the dog's territory and are usually released when the dog defecates. Occasionally these will have to be expressed by hand. Have your veterinarian show you how to do this the first time and then you can do it at home if you choose, even though it is a rather unpleasant job! A sign that the anal glands are clogged is when your dog scoots across the floor on his fanny. On occasion, the glands will appear swollen, which can be seen on a smooth-coated dog.

You also will want to discuss spaying/neutering with your vet. If your PRT is not of show or breeding quality, most vets and breeders recommend this, as it eliminates or reduces the risk of many serious health problems, such as cancers of the reproductive organs. Your vet will advise you about the procedure and the appropriate age to have it done.

YOUR PRT AND HIS VETERINARIAN

Overview

- Ask your breeder or dog-owning friends and neighbors to recommend a good local veterinarian for your PRT.
- There are varying opinions on vaccination protocol, so do some research and discuss your concerns with the vet. Together you should decide on the best way to vaccinate your puppy.
- Acquaint yourself with the PRT's breed-specific health concerns. Some are genetic and some are not, and your breeder should have had his breeding stock tested and certified as free of genetic problems before including them in his breeding program.
- Practice preventative medicine at home with "good housekeeping." Keep your dog clean and always be on the lookout for signs of common dog health issues, as well as any indication of illness or problems. Discuss spaying/neutering with your vet and breeder.

Your Aging PRT

As your dog starts aging, he will also start to slow down. He will not play as hard or as long as he used to and he will sleep and rest more. He will find the sunbeam in the morning hours and take a long nap. At this time, you will probably put him on a senior dog food, but do continue to watch his weight. It is more important than ever not to let your PRT senior citizen become obese. You will notice that his muzzle will start to gray and you may see opacities in his eyes, signs of cataracts.

The aging dog will slow down in his daily activities and will show graying on the muzzle, but will still have that terrier spark.

As your PRT becomes older, he may become arthritic. Continue your walks, making them shorter. Give him a baby aspirin when he appears to be stiff. Keep up with his grooming; both you and he will like to have him looking and smelling his best. Watch for lumps and bumps, and take him to the veterinarian to check out any that you turn up. Incontinence can also become a problem with the older dog. This is frustrating for you and hard on the house, but your dog hasn't become unhousebroken. Rather, his muscle control is fading.

An older dog may seem to forget certain behaviors that once were second nature, but he should never be scolded harshly.

With a terrier, you are blessed with a long-lived dog. PRTs can often be very healthy to 12 to 14 years of age, and it is not unusual for them to live to 15 and 16 years if they have good care.

Veterinary care has changed much over the last decade or two, as has medical care for humans. Your veterinarian can now do much to extend

Senior dogs may become confused more easily and wander into danger, making "old-dog-proofing" as important as puppy-proofing.

your dog's life if you want to spend the money. Unfortunately, this will extend his life, but it will not bring back his youth. Your primary concern should be to help your pet live out his life comfortably. There are medications that can be helpful for this goal. Whatever you decide, try to put your dog and his well-being and comfort ahead of your emotions and do what will be best for your pet.

Always remember the many wonderful years that your Parson Russell Terrier gave to you and your family. With that thought in mind, it may not be long before you are looking for a new puppy or adult PRT for the family. There's no better way to honor your deceased pal than by giving another PRT a good and loving home. And there you are, back at the beginning with a cute bundle of joy, ready for another ten years or more of happiness!

YOUR AGING PRT

Overview

- An aging dog experiences some physical and behavioral changes, most noticeably graying around the muzzle and an overall decrease in his activity level.
- Parson Russell Terriers, and terriers in general, are hardy and blessed with long lifespans, often living well into the double digits.
- Afford your PRT special care and attention in his senior years. Discuss a senior-care program with your vet and make accommodations for the changes that accompany aging.
- Try to make your dog as comfortable as possible in his old age, taking into consideration the many years of happiness and companionship he has given to you.